Poetry Is Not A Written Art

Roland Huff

Compiled by Jude McMurry

Grateful acknowledgment is made to the editors of the following publications in which earlier versions of these poems have appeared: *The Cape Rock*, "Blue China Eyes" (originally titled "Crazy Like a Fox for Anne Sexton"); *DeKalb Literary Arts Journal* , "The Sleeping Dwarf"; *descant* , "My Wild Youth Still Stalks"; *Happiness Holding Tank,* "Formal Ceremonies," "Your Brother Was a Journalism Major"; *Hiram Poetry Review,* "Penelope's Tapestry"; *Long Island Review* , "Genealogy," "That Vast Yellow Ear"; *Phoebe,* "Black Roses"; *Quoin,* "Backstage: The Manager to His Players," "Madonna of the White Magnificat"; *South Dakota Review,* "Against Poems in Celebration of Madness"; *Stonecloud,* "Poetry Is Not a Written Art," "Child's Play" (originally titled "Absurd Dichotomies").

Earlier versions of three poems appeared in the following publications under the pseudonym Kathleen Countess: *Dark Horse,* "Nostalgia"; *Windless Orchard,* "Rocking-Chair Love," "Lai Ancien" (originally titled "Jeanne d'Arc").

Poetry Is Not
A Written Art

CONTENTS

FOREWORD

Roland Kenneth Huff (1942 – 2012) was born in Enid, Oklahoma and grew up in the midwestern U.S., where he was a high school track champion, and in Manchester, England, where his father served as a minister in the mid-1950s. He held a Ph.D. in English from Indiana University, an M.Ed. in counseling psychology from Texas Tech University, and a B.A. in history from Hiram College. As a Rockefeller Fellow, he studied the philosophy of science and religion under Peter Putnam at Union Theological Seminary. For most of his career, he was an associate professor of English at the University of Winnipeg, where despite many battles with his health he specialized in 20th-century American literature, the British novel, science fiction, and the teaching of writing. Prior to that, he directed the graduate and undergraduate programs in rhetoric and composition at Eastern Washington University. He also served on the faculties of Washington State University and the University of Texas at Austin. In his later years, he and his family made their home among the live oaks and bougainvillea of San Antonio, Texas, where he continued to compose poetry and regularly participated in writing workshops. In addition, he developed and practiced a therapeutic counseling approach that he called deep release therapy, which combined elements of talk therapy, hypnotherapy, deep release acupressure, and massage therapy to treat individuals who had emotional trauma.

Those are standard facts. Here is a more telling one: In 1975, to listen to the sound of a brook for a poem he was writing, Roland went for a walk by himself late one evening in an Austin park. Losing the path in the dark, he inadvertently stepped off the edge of a steep limestone cliff and fell straight down twenty-five feet into a boulder-strewn creekbed. He suffered a concussion, multiple broken ribs, two compound fractures of his right arm, and serious back and shoulder injuries. When he regained consciousness several hours later, he got to his feet and somehow staggered upstream in the dark until the slope was shallow enough to climb out of the ravine. He then made his way back to his car and drove himself home to get medical assistance. And he eventually finished the poem.

Over a few short years in his late teens and early twenties, Roland also – as he told it, at least, and leaving out women along the way (which is also how he usually told it) – was voted president of his freshman class, dropped out at midterm to join the army, studied Chinese as a radio intelligence specialist, took a discharge for an existing medical condition, became a bodyguard for several influential Hispanics in southern California who were plotting to overthrow the government of Mexico, prowled the dilapidated factories of Cannery Row while living in a beachside shack in Monterrey, worked as an orderly in the geriatric ward of a women's mental hospital, owned a Jaguar XK140, lived in a mortuary, worked in the men's prison at Walla Walla, hitchhiked repeatedly across the U.S., absorbed Shakespeare through the pores of his skin while dodging bobbies and sleeping in city parks in Stratford-upon-Avon, and lived for weeks in Paris on nothing but cast-off potatoes and onions from the market at Les Halles. Somewhere almost inevitably along that path, he began writing poetry, and he became a thinker, a life-changing teacher, and his own uniquely compelling force, all of it (for years) in a swirl of cigarette smoke.

Like Penelope weaving and unweaving the shroud for Laertes, Roland worked for decades to put together a volume of his poetry but could never draw the line and just say "it is done." Too many new poems, with their own merits, kept coming along. Now, the list is as full as it will ever be. As his wife, typist, editor, reviewer, and occasional muse, I have compiled a selection of the many voices that resonated in Roland's work over a span of nearly fifty years, including work that he composed pseudonymously as a female persona, Kathleen Countess.

Many of these poems would not have happened, or at least would not exist in their revised and stronger forms, without the support and constructive suggestions of a number of Roland's fellow poets in San Antonio who are part of the writing community fostered by Gemini Ink, including his friend Robert Allen and especially the "Wild-Eyed Gang": Cyra Dumitru, Toni Falls, Mariana Aitches Davis, Abbie Cotrell, Celina Villagarcia, Melissa Awbrey, and Jim Heidelberg. Their feedback and Roland's conversations with his long-time poet friend Grace Butcher jump-started a new phase of writing in the last years of his life. Special gratitude and acknowledgment also goes to Marian Haddad, whose keen ear and enthusiastic editing brought a number of Roland's older and somewhat sclerotic poems to life.

There is no formal dedication for this book because, in truth, that decision belonged to Roland, who birthed every page but left no final wishes in this regard. However, from his own drafts of poetry collections, I believe he would have chosen to dedicate this volume to several special people, including (1) the late poet laureate of Hiram College, Hale Chatfield, who Roland said "first taught me what a poem is not"; (2) Roland's oldest friend, Douglas Fisher, who among much other goodness supplied most of Roland's knowledge about gardening and living off the land; (3) Roland's treasured "zen warrior" friend, the late Ray Cook, and (4) most clearly, to the endless joy of our daughter, Dante Elizabeth Huff.

Jude McMurry
April 2015

Poetry Is Not
A Written Art

ECHOES AND VISIONS

Poetry Is Not a Written Art

Poetry is not a written art —
it sleeps on the printed page
like the dream of a woman,
curled up in the mind of a boy.

Poems hibernate in the wombs of vowels,
waiting, like the child, for the rhythms
that will spring out

of darkness, into light.
They lounge idly around
the poles of consonants,

like Galileo restless in Pisa,
without a telescope,
without stars.

Words on the page are Trojan horses
where poetry bides its time
like patient Odysseus,

wreathing his fingers in his awful beard,
until the doorway into time slams down,
and poetry rages off the tongue
to take the unsuspecting city of ourselves.

Backstage: The Manager to His Players

If a player but contrive his entrances and exits cunningly,
may soon be forgotten if he plays the fool between.
So if you have trumpets, let them be borne by pretty pages
and proceed you by eight paces
to voice you as a mighty lord.

Or if you have an old horse,
caparison him in silver to cover up his ribs
and prick him on to rear when you come upon the stage
as if bloody War himself hung upon his tail.

Or let you come solemnly,
like to announce the loss of some great personage,
beating the death march
in slow rolls on sullen drums.

But if you have none of these (as we have none),
you must needs come in the plain fabric of your tale
and like a simple soldier parley with your audience,
as with some great castled town
which you would win with just and equal terms.
So let me hear no swearing of vain oaths,
such as "By God's wounds" or "On my faith,"
for we have not the trappings with which to justify them.

But hark! The audience is without.
Players to your places!
Ring up the curtain!
Let the play begin!

6

That Vast Yellow Ear

Van Gogh
tried to paint the world
like history
(cutting off his ear)
and discovered it a vast negation of light,
but he went on,

Methodically stacking his heavy black lines
into mountains, branching his verticals
into distraught trees, twisting
his percept into his landlady.
  One day borrowing paint from Gauguin,
he discovered color as form:
he painted his black mountains with green snow,
his trees with purple leaves,
his landlady's face orange
— only to discover
that his negation had gone quite mad.

In Arles,
where they confined him
(letting him out during the day to paint),
he paced his stone cell at night
inspecting his mountains and his trees
while defacing his landlady
— until insulted by history
beyond all limits,
he raged up his black mountains
and, pulling his withered ear from his pocket,
nailed it to the canvas.
And it burned.

Genealogy

In 1848
a king of Peru,
a lady of letters,
a lover who shot her,
a wine merchant from Bordeaux,
a Spanish colonel,
drunk one night
(as only the above could be)
all fell together in a feather bed.

The following morning
they left behind
(in the lady of letters)
Gauguin.

Who, as the singular result
of such a composite coupling,
became
a tramp,
a sailor,
a Danish lady's husband,
a stockbroker,
a navvy employed on the Panama Canal,
a bill sticker,
and finally,
after various other avatars,
a painter in Tahiti —

His mind and his primitive
canvases, raging with colors,
notoriously ravaged
by visceral women.

In 1903
the enigma lurking in their eyes
killed him.

Menelaus

Love,
would you put horns upon my head?
And strap me in the useless armor
of an aging Menelaus?
  I am all raging Greek
against that blind beast Time,
who dares to force my bed
and nightly whores me with my love.
If I could grapple with this slippery Paris,
I'd shave him to an early grave.
If I could smell out this thick-walled Troy
I'd burn a million ships along a thousand strands,
and never sleep, nor drink, nor eat
until its towers were dust beneath my feet.

 If one could breach his walls,
what a flood of beauty must pour out
— all the Helens, all the star-crossed lovers,
all the whispered trysts since time began.
  If desire was an act,
I'd burn all time for love,
but as the will falls prey to aging hearts,
even now, love burns for time.
So brief, so sweet, so foolish
like a falling star
that for a single moment
rivals with the moon.

Penelope's Tapestry

Descending from the women's quarters, bare feet mute
on cold stone, naked under the wine-dark robe.
Pausing on the last broad step, heavy, full of dreams,
deciphering time in the half-formed shadows of the raftered hall,
in the final embers of fire and, in the eastern window, dawn.

Stepping into the drunken wreckage of the chamber
— a favorite goblet, chased in silver, crushed
(a hind with hounds in full pursuit) —
heavy timbered tables overturned,
the floor puddled with last night's wine.

Weaving absently among the snoring suitors
towards the door, lifting her robe slightly
from the twitching hands of an uneasy dreamer;
Antinous moans, grazing a single fingernail
against an ankle bone.

Unbarring the heavy doors, slowly easing them ajar,
grey light spilling in, the smell of salt and decaying seaweed,
the barely audible, insistent pulse of waves.
Stealing through quietly like a thief,
turning softly to close the doors.

Stepping through the gates of the house into a sea-mist
morning, a half-hidden world with a dreaming sun.
Unbinding her thick black hair, threaded with silver,
spilling down in heavy waves about her throat,
soaking up the rich, impregnating odor of the sea.

Wandering through the flock of white cackling geese,
escorted, harassed, toward the stone granary
with its long rows of jars and straw-covered floors.
Opening a new storage jar wantonly, just
for the pleasure of breaking the seal.

Using the thumbnail to incise around the lid,
the textured ball of flesh rotating on the smooth stone lip,
the continuous circular ripping of wax revealing
the gaping mouth and golden treasure; gathering up
the thick woolen robe, peasant fashion, into a sower's pouch.

Scooping smooth yellow grains into her wide, child-bearing lap,
heavy rivulets cool against the naked belly underneath, while
around this gleaming island of the sun drapes the golden-threaded
border of the robe, woven ships with oars glistening, sails full-bellied
in the breeze, circling endlessly a woman's land-locked island.

And below it all, beneath the island and the ships,
legs bare almost to the thigh, random grains
spilling down, minute hailstones pelting
her dusty heels, intrudes the impatient,
jealous, hungry gossip of the geese.

Slim, supple necks twining around her calves,
striking quickly at the stray bouncing kernels —
pecking sharply in the small hollows
between the tendons of her toes
for a real or imaginary grain.

Yielding to complaint and numbers,
walking out of the granary,
broadcasting grain in random patterns,
determining the rushes and starts of the geese
by sowing dissension.

Outside, the world no longer dreaming —
the sun burning away the mist,
exposing the empty sea,
minute reflections pricking the eye
from known but unseen waves.

Walking back towards the waking house,
sweat soaking the wisps of hair
behind her ears, trickling down her neck
then beneath the wine-dark robe.
Easing through the heavy gates

To cajole, to threaten, to beg for time,
to plead with the day-burning suitors.

Love and Rape in the King James Version

I

I am a priest, my love,
and I but mask
if I call you love —
for my God, He is a jealous God;
  and has no gods before Him.
Though I am recreant and unfrocked with you,
I hold the power of keys
to bind, to loose, to enter in.
If we are altared here,
it is to His grandeur.

This white rush of you
and this black mane
of your twenty springs
streaming down your white shoulders,
spilling down this subtle river of your back
to pool black jasmine heavy
in the hollow of my loins
is but His winnowing net
strung, woven, tied
in a thousand thousand probabilities
— flung true in design.
  If with this net
He has dredged these night black seas,
seined out the morning and the evening stars,
caught this dreaming moon,
and crammed them
(all that silver, all that gold)
into this room
till the windows shook,
  are we not caught
within this seining of the world,
are we not snared?

II

When I was young and greenly
playful in the grass,
I did not know His name.
I stood naked, unashamed,
in His most holy streams
and thought I laughed the river's rushing
and every string of bubblings to the sea.
The slender grains,
they bent themselves to towel and dry
beneath my small white run
across the fields.
I stood bathed in noonday
and brazen like a wedding bell
announced the sun,
and thought in every golden day
I drove it ringing round the world.

But when I was a man,
He came upon me in the darkness;
He kissed me full and deep
straight on the mouth.
His hands, they took me,
His loins, they knew me,
He burnt his secret name
into the twinings of my bowels,
and I could not bear the Word.

He made of me a bow
and all the world,
it strings me to His hand.
He made of me a lyre —
and every wind
composes Him upon me.
Though I hide in the whispers of the grass,
flee through the valleys,
mute my ears with lead,
fill this mouth with salt,
I but jar and jangle music
with every fleeing step.

III

I am a priest, my love,
and this is not a bed:
It is a hill of elephants
— a den of mountains.
  It is His raging heart
masked in splendour.

Hear then, in dawn
(halfway between sun and moon),
the sudden heron's cry,
the hunting dive of violence.
It is my Lord who hunts,
and what He hunts
is us.
  In this, my unstrung quivering
in your young loins,
again He strings me,
bends me like a bow to His purpose,
and this hot sea
that floods and loosens
all your locks
is but the moving of His finger
as He writes tomorrow
upon us . . .
An accusation of fidelity.

Considering W.B. Yeats (1865 – 1935)

Yeats, you old mad crafter of myths,
did you ever really love a woman?
Or were you always musing —
Cuchulain struggling to govern the tides;

imperfect poet laboring to graft
the immaculate rose upon the rood
of time; Zeus barely skimming
the ground to enfold Leda in the bed

of his white-feathered wings.
So tired of searching for a beauty
crazed as yours, that "dolphin-torn,
that gong-tormented sea,"

you could not even touch
your simple peasant girl.
She tried to read your letters gyred
with poems, the mystic ramblings.

She shook her head in wondering
amusement, stuffed your words in her
apron pocket, went about her business.
And now, as the massive hallway clock

runs out of ticks and tocks, old lecher
of mythologies, sick unto death with desire,
how many dream-tormented returns to
Byzantium? In this last moment, consumed

in the fire of your poems, reduced
to inchoate mumblings, seducer
seduced — was it worth the price
to break, exceed, your grasp?

Christs's Outrageous Beauty [1]

"Cleave the wood and thou shalt find me,
lift the rock and I am there!"
                    from the Gospel according to Thomas

I: Prelude

How far back from
the stark crosses of Golgotha
to Bethlehem? How the journey?
What the price?

No star, no shepherds,
no heralds, no Magi —

Only to discover in an empty
cradle the gaping mouth
of an open tomb.

II: The Garden

SPRING

    Spring-sprung daffodils ache
towards the sun, thrust out of
the rich dark earth, yellow petals lifting
their chins to the noon sky.
    A brown-striped osprey folds her
wings and depth-dives into a calm blue lake,
emerging triumphantly through the ripples
with a silver-flopping fish.
    A bright otter invites exuberance
in her pups, whistles and nudges them
down a long, slippery clay slide
into a shallow, slow-gurgling brook.

---

[1] This is the most complete draft of an unfinished work [JMc]

16

Preparing the Garden

By late March the snow has melted from the kitchen garden, 20 feet by 30 feet. On the fence posts, he staples an eight-foot deer fence, while earthworms still curl tightly three feet underground.

On the first weekend of April, he drives his old pickup truck twenty miles to an abandoned chicken ranch and digs out chicken shit in two-foot trenches. Arriving home, he tills the droppings deeply into the black moist soil.

In mid-April, he uses a hoe to craft straight furrows with small hillocks between them. He plants early crops: butter lettuce, escarole, spinach, radishes, green onions, small cabbages. He rakes up shallow mounds and places seven or eight seeds for melons, cucumbers, and zucchini in six of them. In three others he stakes up small seedling tomatoes. He spreads straw on the mounds to discourage the weeds.

Spring Reprise

Out in the hill country, there is a limestone
spring swelling up into the trill of a stream
that rushes downhill, dropping as small
waterfalls into shallow sandy pools.
  The stream is remote, a guarded secret,
but he bathes there naked in early May
when the waterfalls and pools are surrounded
by an earth-hosted mist of blue lupines.

* * * * *

At Auschwitz in the end they threw living children into the ovens and made lampshades of human skin. Christ went into the ovens with every child, taking every cyanide shower, standing in trenches to be shot in mass graves.

The hearts of Hiroshima and Nagasaki simply evaporated. Christ became a blackened silhouette on a Japanese bridge, annihilated with a hundred thousand elderly, housewives, and children. His flesh sloughed off in great open sores and filled, over the next thirty years, all the deformed babies.

SUMMER

The bougainvillea, splayed against a white-washed wall,
flaunts the magenta leaves surrounding tiny white blossoms.
Industrious bees stuff pollen into leg sacs.

A twenty-foot fountain surges vertically, pauses, then
splashes down in rippling circles. Golden shadows of old carp
glide back and forth beneath the many colors of the water lilies.

Four kittens growl and charge and gnaw in mock
and real battle; they jostle and shoulder one another
into a pile on their mother's belly, noisily suckle and knead,
then fall into a perfect sleep.

Planting and Harvesting

In the first weeks of June, he picks lettuce and spinach daily.
He strips ten-foot lodgepole pines, tying them together
in threes to form small teepees, then sows under each
ten of his great-grandmother's Kentucky Wonder beans.

In early summer, he is still planting corn kernels weekly,
three inches apart, so that rows of fresh ears ripen over
an extended period; meanwhile, he is starting to harvest
green onions, radishes, and carrots.

In midsummer, he waters and gathers. Most days he weeds
for half an hour in a meditative trance. He mounts a large
Blue Bird sprinkler on a four-foot post in the center of the garden.
The tcuk, tcuk, tcuk, tcuk waters the entire plot.

In August, he harvests for more than an hour each day:
sacks of new potatoes, paper bags of cucumbers, endless
cartons of zucchini, bushels of brandywine tomatoes —
tithes of abundance for the homeless shelter.

Summer Reprise

Heat-veined lightning stalks fitfully through the low, gray clouds
on the far horizon of the dry land. Towering black thunderheads
slowly rise up, rumbling like cannons.

Lightning begins to detonate in strikes near the house.
A hundred-year-old oak is riven of a huge limb. Then, finally,
the sweet summer rain begins to splash on his calm, raised face.

* * * * *

There are 58,191 names carved on the black granite wall, among our most visibly honored dead. But when their lives were taken, barely half the nation decried their youthfulness, an average age of 23. Christ perished with each raw draftee, ordered to engage an enemy inseparable from the indigenous people for whom they fought.

Christ stumbled, sweating and terrified, in the rice paddies of foreign jungles. He returned crippled and ignored, spat upon and called a baby killer. Isolated by post-traumatic stress, Christ became just one more of the addicted, aging homeless.

FALL

Monarch butterflies on their passage to Mexico pause overnight, settle by the thousands on a young, bare tree. Morning light reveals a cathedral of stained glass wings.

Immense pink-silver salmon, improbably leaping staircases of waterfalls, return to their mother streams. Their powerful tails thresh out hollows in the gravel: spawning, fertilizing, dying.

With a clatter of interlocked antlers, two resplendent stags rear and charge into one another, again and again, until the elder, bloodied, driven to his knees, abandons the does.

Final Harvesting

The cornucopia of the garden continues late into September. He is still giving away tomatoes, cucumbers, and mounds of zucchini. The harvest of many tubers and pumpkins may go on until the first hard frost, as late as mid-November. He strews the mounds deeply with insulating straw.

In a last pass through the garden, he wraps in newspaper individual Idaho potatoes, carrots, and turnips. He places them in separate boxes, walks down the steep stairs of the root cellar, and storages them on shelves. Sweet onions hang from the rafters.

One task remains: the plucking of the firm, ripened Jonathan apples on the old, sixty-foot garden tree. Neighbors and friends hauling tall ladders arrive after lunch on Saturday, buckets attached to their belts.

Fall Reprise

    His great-grandfather's white oak cider press is five feet
high at the rear end; there is a wooden hopper into which
the apples are poured by the bushel into the oaken barrel.
The grinder, with its combined slicing blades and pressure
plate, is a huge screw which fits into the oak barrel.
    It takes two people to turn the screw handles. With thermoses
of coffee and tea, a small group returns to help. By late afternoon,
they have pressed ninety gallons. His friends disperse, spent,
with their wine jugs full of the raw apple cider.

* * * * *

Pearls of oil, baked for millenia in ancient rocks, pour into the
oceans from offshore drilling rigs lit up like casinos. Factory
wastes sludge into streams and rivers. The land parches; the
tundra melts; the oceans steam and acidify.

Christ falters as the great blue currents of the sea can no longer
purge the pollution that propagates the growth of toxic algae.
The devastating red tides do not obey the push and pull of the
moon. Christ is entombed in bleached and lifeless coral reefs.

WINTER

    The early sun uncovers diamonds of hoar frost on each separate
twig and makes the air sparkle. Delicate crystals etch the windows
with icy lace: ferns, flowers, feathers, faces, and geometric forms.
    A white snowshoe hare nibbles on dry rose hips from a wild
briar bush. Suddenly she is aware of a red fox, ten feet away,
tracking by scent. The hare bolts, but the vixen is too fast,
effortlessly breaking the neck and dragging the crimson-stained
body back to her kits.
    A wolf pack gathers at their rendezvous point. They frolic and
roll in the snow until a prolonged deep growl from the alpha wolf
signals the hunt. When the prey is slain and gorging is over, the pack
begins to yip and howl, drawn-out symphonies, cellular at the bone.

Preparing for Winter

The trees have shed their last gallimaufry blazons of color.
Their limbs stand like gaunt skeletons against the horizon. He
takes five gallons of cider laced with yeast down to the old root cellar
to ferment.

In late November, he begins the garden clean-up with a honed
World War II machete, chopping through the old vines and stalks,
with the exception of three rows of Indian corn.

The next weekend, he roughly tills the wilted remains of the garden
into the soil. The first gentle snow blows in across the big lake, falling
like feathers on his outstretched tongue.

At midnight on the winter solstice, he steps into the root cellar and
brings up a gallon of thick fermented cider. A single swallow freezes
his throat and thaws his heart. Stars and constellations wheel about
him in the dark.

He utters a great shout: "I SEE, I SEE THE GARDEN."

Winter Reprise

At dusk, three does and a late fawn drift down
like smoke through the silence of the Ponderosa pines
and the heavily falling snow.

The deer fence removed, the does move carefully
to the three rows of Indian corn planted for them
in July — first a nibble, then the powerful, hungry
crunching of the hard kernels.

* * * * *

In underground cellars, electric wires are attached to Christ's
testicles and he writhes and screams and screams. All sides
take a turn at his torture; their techniques vary, but the agony is
the same. Precisely at noon on Christmas Eve, a jihadi
terrorist carries the inevitable nuclear suitcase bomb into
Rockefeller Center Plaza, and half of Manhattan goes 9/11.

Christ stumbles exhausted through the shelled rubble of dusty
towns. Emaciated, orphaned children approach him and ask
in Arabic, "Can you take care of me?"

III: A Christology of Evolution

If flesh came into being because of spirit,
that is a marvel, but if spirit came into being
because of the body, that is a marvel of marvels.
                    from the Gospel according to Thomas

The divine spark
at the beginning,
now revealed
by consciousness
. . . .

A DIFFERENCE IN POETIC TRADITIONS

The Great Shout of Noon

The flat rock
cleaves the middle of the river,

a ship's prow breasting
the currents, fixed, immovable.

Cruciform, I occupy this space,
spread-eagled to the sun,

naked on my back, laid out
on the great hearth.

Light melts into bones
pulses through radiating

limbs, dances in the blood,
surges through the chambers

of the heart, spills out
of my mouth in the great

shout of noon — *Kai!*[2] —
here, now.

---

[2] A Japanese word for *spirit*, sometimes voiced explosively in a
moment of spiritual enlightenment

Formal Ceremonies

the white sun
suspended in the morning mist
burns through the bamboo groves

the silence of my love
squatting on the stone floor
nude thighs askew
splashing into a white bowl

water boiling for our tea
mats rolled and placed in a corner
and after green tea
I will sandal my feet
I will walk into our garden
I will contemplate the red hibiscus
(raging by the pool)
and meditate upon the golden carp
moss-encrusted
browsing among the roots of water lilies

Gliding into Zen

I run through warm green summer rain
around the old-fashioned cinder track

Listening to my breathing, relaxing
the calf muscles on the down-swing.

Surprisingly calm, my breathing slows
as I increase the length of my stride.

A sparkling moment strips
twenty years away as I begin to float

Down the backstretch with that effortless
glide that cannot be taught.

Kai!

Medicine Woman

For Jan Jarboe Russell

The wrinkled, grey-haired Hopi
woman with her bright black eyes
is impervious to heat at ninety-two.
She soaks up the sun like young
ferns soak up the rain.

She drapes her hand-woven shawl
across her bony shoulders,
puts on her yellow bonnet,
opens the worn screen door
and sits in her one bleached chair.

She relaxes into the pounding
afternoon light and drifts into
her nap, not a cloud in the
endless blue sky, framed
only by a distant butte.

Soon the heat takes her in
a dreaming sleep of wild
horses and antelope, then
deeper to a darker journey.
After several hours, she stirs

and begins to open her eyes
— a warning rattle, and
she feels the heavy weight
of the large snake coiled
in the warmth of her lap.

The rattler flicks its tongue
in and out, poised to strike.
The old woman muses,
drowsy, what a strange way
to pass to the other side.

She relaxes back into the sun
and soon is lost and found
again in sleep. As the first
shadows from the porch fall
across the chair, she floats gently

back to this world.
The spirit snake is gone.
Was she the messenger?
Was she the message?

Love Feast: A Prose Poem for Anne Sexton

Scene I: The poet in his study, ten days after her death

6:00 A.M. The first heavy snow swirling down in the dark.
Mourning is the hardest grief.

> Died. Anne Sexton, 45, suburban housewife who turned
> to poetry during a nervous breakdown 18 years ago and
> proceeded to write seven books of searingly personal
> verse, including the Pulitzer-prizewinning *Live or Die*
> (1966); apparently by her own hand (carbon-monoxide
> inhalation); in Weston, Mass. Clearly intrigued in her
> poems by the thought of her own death, Sexton survived a
> number of suicide attempts.
>   *Time Magazine*, October 14, 1974

Sitting before the gaping tomb of your obituary. Staring blankly
into a glass paperweight ("The New England Glass Company;
East Cambridge, Mass; circa 1900; a classic introduction of three-
dimensional form into blown glass"): a Boston street in winter,
crafted in turn-of-the-century rusty brick, framed with iron
railings. Invert the crystal ball. Replace it exactly in the center
of your death.

Scene II: Interlude, a snowy afternoon in Boston

Laundry baskets of snow shaken out, tires spinning on the
slippery street — two awkward, aging children suddenly retrieving
innocence down a sidewalk glaze of ice, clutched and interwound,
jockeying in jerks of rescue, starts of disaster. Your laughter
like crystal bells.

Victors accusing, confessing self-preservation. Survivors
staggering down the subterranean stairs to Mama Eleni's,
bursting through the door, snow-flurried, helpless in laughter,
abruptly hushed, in the wash of candlelight, by the vibrant melody
from a santouri. Snow sparkling, melting in your rich brown hair.

Suddenly remembered strangers in each other's arms; measuring
out the awkward silence. Social readjustments. Fugitives from
the same faculty lecture, our only introduction a passing acquaintance

with one another's poems. Mama Eleni's youngest son appearing
to lead us through a host of candles and white starched tablecloths
to a secluded corner. No one else but Mama Eleni, monitoring
the shortwave radio behind the bar; nothing but santouri.

Amber-shadowed retsina in the wine glass, deceptively smooth,
silken, flaring into resinous fire, flaunting the after-hint of anise.
Laughter about playing hooky from the "Psycho-Social Implications
of Victorian Pteridemania"; truant burlesques of the academic
beast. Establishing perimeters: casual chatter about students
and teaching, acknowledgment of mutual acquaintances, passing
comments on the economic straits of the small reviews.

Drifting with the retsina from the rumored execution of
The Kenyon Review into ars poetica — your definition woven
with slender, articulate hands: "The art of listening to your
self, and screaming with precision or loving or dying."
Agreeing, "No one ever learns to write a poem. One only learns
what a poem isn't." Cresting, palms lifted, at the figures a poem
makes into celebration (your pale blue eyes catching fire):
the quicksilver music of John Donne's "go and catch a falling star,"
the consummate mystery of W.B. Yeats' "that dolphin-torn,
that gong-tormented sea," the inconceivability of Dylan Thomas'
"the force that through the green fuse drives the flower."

Suddenly aware, in candlelight and shadows, of surrounding
conversations; the clatter of dishes and silverware; the odors
of roasted meats, spices, herbs; Mama Eleni's sons hurrying back
and forth to the kitchen. Perimeters established and over-run.
Awkward checking of watches; recitations and comparisons of
responsibilities and mealtimes. Respite; decision. Telephone calls
to respective spouses. Proceeding you back to the table, catching
the eye of Mama Eleni's youngest son, more retsina and our desire
for menus. Watching you return through the crowded room,
your hair freshly brushed, your face lighting up in welcome.

Laughing over the menu's ambiguous gloss of the house salad:
"Diphilus, the respected ancient Greek physician, considered lettuce
inhibiting to the sexual drive, but that didn't stop the hedonistic
philosopher Aristoxenus from watering the lettuce in his garden
with wine and honey." Deciding we might as well be hung for it all —
roast lamb with artichokes, dolmathes, and kalamata olives.

Mama Eleni's youngest son appearing to take our order,
reappearing with sesame-encrusted koulouri rolls and the
ambiguous salad: lettuce crisp and finely cut, anointed with olive
oil and lemon, tossed with moist crumbles of fresh feta cheese,
budded with fat purple olives. Libations to Aristoxenus;
casual gossip about ourselves, our families, trying to explain
what a poet is to a four-year-old, the problems of growing up as
an awkward child, commemorating old friends, Sylvia Plath.

Mama Eleni's youngest son arriving with the sacrificial
lamb, anointed with olive oil, oregano, and lemon, incised and
impregnated with garlic, spitted and turned over an open fire;
artichokes steaming and unflowering; dolmathes and olives.
Mock accusations, confessions of seduction from pre-thawed
hamburger, children to kiss goodnight, and lectures to prepare.
Dithyrambs of santouri ... and your pale blue eyes.

Teasing, cajoling one another into ancient Greek customs,
tearing the seared and roasted meat by hand, fingers scorching
in the hot inner flesh. Time losing course in the fusing tributary
currents — spices and herbs mingling in the savours of flesh and
the succulent base of the artichoke leaf, merging in retsina,
confluence and time flooding into the shimmering moment.

Byzantine dolmathes — sensuous packets of ground and highly
seasoned beef; wild rice, currants, and walnuts; spiced with
cinnamon; splashed with port wine; neatly rolled, tucked, and
bound in grape leaves. Intimations of Dionysus — this is my body
unrobed for you. Contemplating your long, oil-slickened fingers
subtly stripping the artichoke, leaf by leaf.

The lithe tongue's caress of purple olives; sharp teeth
slow in the soft, tart flesh; reflecting on the irreducible
center — Athena flowering in the rotting brain. Laughter in our
wanton feasting ... your candled face inclining to me,
the lightest touch of your fingertips fingers on my exposed wrist.

Removing the last leaf from the artichoke, devouring the
final grape leaf. Finger-bowls; your languid fingers dripping
rose water ... Mama Eleni's youngest son appearing to clear the
table. Neither of us desiring dessert — but of course kafedaki,
and Cambas brandy.

Alternating between the semi-sweet of the coffee and the fire
of the Cambas; basking in the intimate silence like subtle cats.
Reluctantly owning time. Catching the eye of Mama Eleni's
youngest son; paying the bill; dispatching him to call your cab.
Cherishing the last of the Cambas, savouring the shimmering
candlelight and the last measures of silence between us.

Mama Eleni's youngest son appearing to inform us that your
taxi has arrived. Outside the night is bitter cold but crystal
clear. Intertwined like old lovers, climbing up the icy stairs
from Mama Eleni's. Releasing me, lifting your face upwards,
your hair spilling back, your slender hands gesturing up
into the dark — "Oh starry, starry night!" Handing you
into the cab. The driver turning, "Where to, lady?"

Scene III: Evening of the same day, the poet still in his study

It is getting dark again here, Anne. The snow has stopped falling.
Time losing course in the wake of your passage, the day has been
spent, retrieved, spent, in mourning labour. Snow-bound in your
absence, I read my death; snow-bound in your poems, I read my life.

Did you really think that we could let you go? You have no
choice but to survive. Time is a vacant death notice —

> Always, sweet Anne,
> dear Anne, mad Anne,
> you candle me,
> kindle, and cajole me;
> sweeten me,
> swive, and seduce me;
> threaten, thieve,
> and thigh-me;
> mischief-kiss
> and lure me
> always, sweet Anne,
> dear Anne,
> mad Anne.

Black Roses
for Nikki Giovanni

Fierce, emaciated poet,
scorched to the bone in
rage.

You image a city father's
boogie dream, another
smoldering summer night,
another four–alarm
fire.

Consuming black blossom
death–fused slow burn
in darkling streets,

Latent
molotov rose,
nightstick fired
in summer lightning

— detonating in gunfire
erupting in riot–
splintering glass,
a hell–hole flower

Full blown and furnaced,
death–stoked
and self–consuming
rose.

Sweet incendiary poet,
throw your honkie,
cocktailed audience
another dozen short–fused,
black American beauty
poems —

Live grenades
        bouncing
                across the floor.

The Awakening

Like some great Yeatsian bell tolling
fathoms deep beneath the sea, I rouse
upwards, slowly, from the wreckage of my
suicidal dreams — to find myself curling
around your naked buttocks. I slip
my left hand around your shoulder and
cradle a full breast with the nipple
caught between my first and second fingers.

I grow tumescent and gently knead your
breast, like the warm dough of fresh
bread, until the nipple grows hard.
I slide between your thighs; you sigh and
shift your legs, pushing back against me.
Easily I slip inside you, like eternity,
and both of us, half awake, rock, rock,
rock into morning. This is how I want to live.

Blue China Eyes

for Anne Sexton

Mischief witch
and mistress

drag me, spell me
in your crazy house

I want to play and
wanton with

disordered, broken
nightmare toys.

Sensual, mad
poppet – I want

to finger and tongue
you, back through

childhood's
shattered pale

blue china
eyes.

On the road to Bedlam
and part way back,

climbing nightmares
of Rapunzel hair

these eighteen years;
madness is

the only cure:
crazy, crazy, crazy

fired and furnaced
like a fox in heat.

Requiem for a Poet Still Living

Falstaff
regretting Hal,
grizzled beard, broken shoulders
hulking over monstrous sagging gut,
standing on a cliff-hung terrace
surrounded by the literati,

hefting his ponderous,
poem-wrinkled phallus
toward the moon,
splashing, pissing
over the ledge of rock,
streaming star fire
into the darkness below,
roaring, "NIAGARA!"

. . . but ah, sweet prince.

Homophobic Solitary Confinement

Why is this
a house of all men?
(I can hear them rocking softly
in their solitary beds)

If this is
a house of all men,
somewhere there must be
a house of all women

And each moans out
in the need for love
(I can hear the spasm rock them
in their solitary beds)

A Difference in Poetic Traditions

You told me
you told one of your friends
I was somewhat of a poet,

And she assumed
I was a quiet, reserved,
Robert Lowell sort of a person

Whereas, I assumed
she would have assumed
I was a raunchy son of a bitch,

Braying lustily at women
half my age; belching up
poems like Jonah brought
forth from the whale; scratching
the hairy armpits of my experience
and farting fire.

I really want to meet
your friend. If she can
fantasize about Robert Lowell
fantasizing about gang
banging the Hell's Angels
— we'll get along just fine.

Your Brother Was a Journalism Major

You said,
your brother was a journalism
major, but in the war he painted
tanks (steely death on tracks, rumbling
from the woods, waking the sleepy village
— blitzkrieg).

I said,
so nice of the army
to give him
a job (sixty millimeter guns, long
and needle-deadly, piercing the foliage
— camouflage).

You said,
oh, no. Not those
kind of tanks. Storage
tanks (smoke curls from the wreckage,
tread marks across the park
— retraction).

10:20 Flight to L.A.

What first appeared a falling star
was but a loosened wire,
a careless mechanic turning silver wings
to fire against the night,
tumbling towards a pastured sea.

A shining dream of birds
exploding in a grotesque arabesque
of acrobatic dolls, erratic pantomimes of flight
that fail and fall into the net of gravity:

Luggage dances, pinwheels, bounces through the grass,
bursting like giant seedpods into multi-colored blossoms,
and all the time, a strange spring rain of sunglasses,
briefcases, shoes, a blonde wig,
fragments of metal thud,
tinkle, splinter into the meadow.

Slim pale leg
white blossom wantons
in the deep, wet grass
between a shock-proof watch
and a glossy black laptop —
lacing them with red arterial fingers
into a chance collage of death
        — until the men from town arrive
and, sweating over nudity/white blossom/
sweep up the jigsaw puzzle
        so that the experts
may piece together the severed
and the scattered,
reconstruct the shattered,
correlate the isolated,
        and thus determine
why time is shock-proof,
and gleaming laptops still hold poems,
when life no longer runs
on slim white legs of love.

Four Square and Sturdy Like a Union Jack
for Catherine's father

Well, now your father's gone
the old blustering Tory, who celebrated
Victoria's birthday and sang
"God Save the Queen," lowered
into the grave with a Union Jack
draped over the coffin.

The primal Canadian,
who fled the new-found land in fear
of some ancient shipwrecked sin,
but made the pilgrimage back
in penance once a year,
telling tales to a small Catherine
of such boyhood storms they had to open
all the doors and windows wide to let
the thunder and the lightning roar
straight through the house.

The out-of-date patriot,
who, when asked by a young Catherine
how many Germans he had killed, replied,
"God knows, Cath, I pray not a one.
I fired the gun in th' air
and hoped they'd run like hell."

The gentle, determined man,
who stopped his car and traffic
in both directions to carry an irritable
antediluvian snapping turtle across
the road and down to a stream,
returning with a handkerchief wrapped
around a savaged thumb, reflecting
"You know, Cath, some people
steer out of their way
to hit them."

God knows, how could such a large man die?
Two hundred and eighty pounds, and the coffin bearers strained.
God knows, you have lowered him into the grave;

God knows, you face an ambivalence of grief.
But hold your doors and windows open
to let his voice keep rumbling through.

"Cath, how about another
cuppa tea?"

Zucchini Child
for Hannah at 13 months

Zucchini-child
harvesting the summer sun
in a profusion of vines
and yellow blossoms

Encroaching across
the ordered rows
of your mother's
third novel

By fall, we will have to
give you away
in baskets
to the neighbors

Little Black Burro

Death is a
little black burro
who comes to my back door
each night.

I curry his curly
coat and hand-feed
him carrots and tell
him good night.

One night I am going
to bring him into the
house as a special
guest and after the carrots

I am going to get up on him
with my feet dragging
on the ground

And ride out through the
front door and never
return.

The Sleeping Dwarf
(A Parable for Scholars)

Evening, a track of lanterns up the mountainside; just before dawn, a track of lanterns down. Dozing all day; every night delving in the mountain's heart; plundering the sleeping fires of diamonds, emeralds, rubies; garnering moonstones, bloodstones, opals; hoarding lapis lazuli, jasper, jade. It's not a bad profession being a dwarf.

But the caverns are damp, the hours are long, and you tend to lose track of time. It's bad even to wonder what the weather's like outside; that's when your pick slips. Don't think about it much, though; one becomes accustomed to one's schedule. But when I begin to speculate what the season is, I know it's time to take a break from the job, go sit by the fire (or is it summer?), smoke a clay pipe, heft a stein, and do a little wood carving. When you see faces and cunning beasties in the cavern walls, that's the flickering of the torchlight. But when they start that damn whispering when you turn your back, it's time to get out for a while.

Besides, I have the feeling I ought to spend some time with Snow White. She's been a little restless lately; probably that damn Prince Charming slinking about the woods again, always trying to smirk around you with his good manners. (The blasted gigolo! Probably never worked a day in his life — nothing better to do than ride a bloody great white horse through the woods. Can't control the beast anyway; last week, broke through the picket fence and trampled half the vegetable garden). But, certainly, she's off her feed; hasn't seemed overly impressed with the last few wheelbarrows of precious stones, either.

I admit the diamonds haven't been of the first water lately, but you have to take the bad with the good, and the sapphires have been exceptional this year, and certainly there's not a princess in the kingdom who has a trousseau like our Snow White. Of course, she's got to wait for the right man to come along, and about all we get around here is Prince Charming (and who would sweep the house? cook the food? make the beds? put out the cat?) —

Aaah, but I'm a worrier. After all, Prince Charming is a harmless enough fool who couldn't discover the castle gate if he was mounted on the drawbridge. I've just been shut in the same cavern with the same six other dwarves too long. Not all dwarves are clean. It's the little things that bother you, personal habits. It's not the sneezing that gets to you, it's the constant sniffling while you wait for the sneeze.

46

But I have this sense of apprehension, and my arthritis has been flaring up the last few days. Either it's been raining a lot outside, or else that damn witch is up to something new. Always has a con going: "No money down! Satisfaction guaranteed!" I can tell when it's going to be one of those weeks; I get the same pain, just here, in the lower back. First it was the comb, then the corset — I wonder what she's giving away this time? And that nitwit Snow White would buy life insurance from a dead man just to pass the time of day. Walks around in a daze half the time.

Maybe the answer is a little trip. Let Snow White break out a few geegaws from the vault. (She's always complaining she can't even wear them. Woman's point of view, of course. Nothing like precious stones to hold their value for your old age.) Trek into town, do a little camping on the way; she'd like that. See the castle; probably a fair going on. She's never been to the diamond exchange. Buy her a new dress; keep her away from the princes. But somehow, I'm not altogether sure that Snow White and overwork are all the problem and that going to town is all the answer. It's probably just middle-age anxiety, damp caverns, and arthritis of the spine; maybe I'll feel better tomorrow night.

Yet I've seen a lot of dwarves come and go — you can't stay away from the caverns too long, or you begin to get bigger. And I always remember what my father said, when he left the mines: "Even dwarves, inordinately crafting, cunning, and inquisitive as they are, have to grow up sometimes."

POEMS COMPOSED AS KATHLEEN COUNTESS

Lai Ancien

Jeanne D'Arc
Died May 30, 1431

May auto-da-fe,
You a bright bouquet
Scorched.
Tryst day, passion play,
Now Christ's chevalier
Torched.

    -- Kathleen Countess

Child's Play

Man,
that hairless leper,
slunk into the dream,
dragging the short stump of his sword behind.

Squatting on his haunches,
he inspected the protruding bones of his feet
and scratched his scabs,
scattering scales upon the floor
(which he picked up
and put in his pocket,
to make a fish with later).

Meanwhile the dream and I,
taking no notice of this intruder,
played out our game of chess
with bluebells,
while young colts
    romped staccato across the board
        upsetting all our calculations
           in a profusion
              of petals.

  -- Kathleen Countess

Ars Poetica

A typical argument between
William Carlos Williams
and Wallace Stevens
on an ordinary Sunday
afternoon:

On main street
nothing is happening
(out of the ordinary).

Three naked women
are sleeping on top
of the courthouse cupola
(six white breasts arranged
tastefully among them).

What if we dressed them
in red nightgowns,
and no one noticed?

What if I composed
this poem
in a red nightgown
(my remaining breast
artfully concealed)?

      -- Kathleen Countess

Nostalgia

(And now,
    the news...)

A General Electric clock
radio computes 7:00 A.M.
and I awaken, in your arms,
to a preview of the world.

The Viet Cong have infiltrated
my red nightgown, launching
a major attack upon the white
provinces of my breasts.

Your tongue sidles down
the Ho Chi Min trail, slips
quietly into the jungle,
contravenes the DMZ.

President Nixon states America
will never abandon its commitments,
while your fingers are acting as
unindicted co-conspirators.

Early negotiations are underway
to select, as I roll sideways,
advantageous positions
around the Paris peace table.

Meanwhile, in the Middle East,
Israeli forces have crossed
the Suez Canal, and the troops
are driving deep into Egypt.

Finally, someone somewhere has
pushed that secret red button,
and the world blazes apart
again, and again, and again.

    -- Kathleen Countess

Language Lessons

They say it takes
as long to forget
a foreign language
as it took
to learn it.

Six years married to you
(counting one before, seven loving).
Does that mean, in seven years,
I will be free?

Really? And will the world be
my carousel again? Oh! That horse!
or that horse! Or this horse
would be fine! Will I catch
the brass ring,
again?

In seven simple years, will I
no longer turn to you in morning
dreams, and murmur,
"Hold me..."?

-- Kathleen Countess

Professor at Menopause

You have made a profession
out of stage-managing
your three-piece suit
and your limited research.

You seldom attend
a conference session unless
you are giving a paper,
trotting out your stale ideas
with new classroom anecdotes,
but you never miss
a social event, and you
are all too familiar a scene
at the cash bar.

You stalk the convention halls
like an arthritic, aging
predator, scanning the crowd
for female graduate students
or an older woman
who might be flattered
by the attentions of a scholar.

Every time you look at me,
it's like a wrinkled hand
sliding into my underwear.

    -- Kathleen Countess

LOVE, LOSS, HEALING

Coming Back After a Serious Injury

Acrobatic alchemists of pain,
like a cripple on a trampoline,
you learn to push off harder
with the twisted leg.

Relearn the fundamentals,
bound and rebound. Recalculate
the torque and thrust of simple
spins and twists.

So, you begin again;
life ebbs back
in sweat and practice,
a thousand almost perfect

Moves, until one night,
a little drunk, the stars
too close, you try an absolute
back-layout double,

Spin constellations twice
about a solid center,
and find yourself
once more in flight —

The death-defying
double-backwards
somersault
of love.

The Logic of Cherry Blossoms

. . . a conversation overheard in Washington Square

I love to hear you dissect
the meaning of our quarrels, dear,

and searching for my pipe
is not a mere stratagem

to delay the argument
into philosophy.

But as we walk
through the pastel logic

of these cherry blossoms,
down the syllogism of this street,

let us not forget
the universe is ruled by law.

We, like blossoms,
compound inevitabilities,

are but the conclusion
of an assertion far wider

than our own. And spring does not
necessarily dance in the stiletto heels

of a woman's presuppositions,
but firmly treads a deeper rhythm

in the blood — which leads me
to the fact that it was physics — not I

that sent the young girl's skirt
swirling around her buttocks.

Your comment —
that I got that heavy, bull-male look

and all but pawed the ground,
it seems to me is — excessive.

Your assertion
that if the mind has mental hands,

I am a kleptomaniac, plucking blossoms
somewhat indiscriminately

— perhaps is true.
But, it was the wind — not I,

that flipped up her skirt
and exposed me, already delving

between her thighs —
And if the logic of the cherry blossoms

did not provoke a certain fever in the blood;
and if the wind was not as lecherous as thought —

it is altogether more than possible
I might have never touched you

with these more than mental hands.

Rocking Chair Love

I have a dream
of a perfect rocking chair...

I've never seen it,
but I'll know it
    when I see it.

I'll just sit right down,
and say, "Honey, rock me,
rock me to death."

And then I'll take
it home.

Poetic Joyride in the Royal George Hotel

As we sit here killing oysters
and a pedestrian bottle of white wine
in the quiet afternoon of the bar,

I bypass the usual forms
of ignition, hotwiring your mind
with a poem scribbled on a napkin.

Speeding down your open freeways,
clover-leafing in metaphor
towards the junction of your thighs,

It occurs to me: Policemen
are real, and the drunken
drivers are myself.

Red lights flashing on
and off — spell out
a cheap hotel.

Madonna of the White Magnificat

It is time to spread your thighs again.
The world drives me home,
this crazy scheme of things
that signs you as desire
in each friend's dreaming flesh
but leaves me cold.
What I investigate in you
is a different, distant fire,
like through a telescope refracting,
laser, white magnificat.

What I discover
in your nameless heart
is old and white, supernal
as an arctic landscape
cloaked in darkness
— a single star
exploding nova
a thousand years ago
— another hundred thousand years
before illumination.

EXmas

And so we celebrate
this Christmas Eve — epiphany,
divorce. Amid some talk of Caesar,
tax returns, and property
Settlements,

Casually sundering flesh from
flesh, we divide the myrrh
and frankincense and gold.
It is a hard and brutal
Birth.

The stars are distant
in this cold stable.
Impotent magi, we celebrate
the passing of the
Coming.

Against Poems in Celebration of Madness

And for all the flickering torchlight
beauty of monastic cells, the flooding
moon stranding silver flopping stars upon
my bed, the wolf's visionary snarl, and my
insane heart running naked through the
cobbled streets, I would not go that way
again.

It was a carnival, a capering hunch
back dwarf, a tight wire act with mirrors,
a grotesque crystal ball of pickled
embryos, a tattooed lady blushing purple
roses, a dragon flagged against the night
in fire, but I would not go that way
again.

It was a crazy, whirling carousel of
words, a musical extravaganza; I rode a
pie eyed horse, a spavined, sway backed
stallion; I roweled him on in place
until the wheeling night bled coagulated
stars, but I would not go that way
again.

I have been mad,
and it wears me like a promise.

Reflecting on a Female Physician

If I were to fall again
from a high place,
splintered to wrack and ruin
on the rocks below,

I can imagine myself
in your slender, articulate hands:
your quiet voice murmuring
as you move amidst the surgical
clutter of my repair, counselling
repose — prescribing hope, release
from pain, long-awaited sleep
and dreams.

I discover myself
like some dumb beast of burden
driven beyond its limits, lying
down at last in the healing
comfort of your touch.

My life is too vulnerable
to be left solely in the hands
of men.

The Gift-Child
For Dante Elizabeth, at 3 months

You did not drop mindlessly
like an apple. Five years

of sperm counts
in solitary
changing rooms,

imagining lust
in the immediate vicinity
of strangers;

cameras of light
inside your mother's womb
tracing the labyrinth
of fallopian tubes;

love-labor
by the tidal schedules
of the moon,
toiling
upon each other's body.

You should know
that you were
passion's child —
a one-night, momentary retreat
from middle age,

a sweat-drenched mounting
dissolving into
the brutal comfort
of the maimed.

In this interminable stage
of menopausal rage,
you were
an autumn storm
on a clear night
with a full moon —

Lightning
stalking across
the barren fields,
sweet rain,

and the seed took
inconceivable root.

Oh, no, you
were not mindless
as an apple falling.
You
are the gift
-child.

My Wild Youth Still Stalks

My wild youth still stalks
somewhere in the hills.
Now and then, on a clear day,
you can see him hurling boulders out to sea.

So it is the boundaries and the limits
are staked out.
But more and more,
I stay home of nights

and when I awaken in your arms
to hear his wild fantastic fluting in the rain,
I drowsily smile and curl more deeply
into you, and quietly celebrate the night

in the least discovery of your hand
as you move to find me in the dark.

The Blessèd Rain

The enclosed patio forms part of our house;
    three large brick columns
and wrought-iron arches and bars uphold
    the front roof. A brick wall encases
the heavy oak front door. The wrought
    iron gate frames the entry—the passage,
like a Mexican jail, a barred door,
    a security lock. Doctors' orders insist
I lead a confined life.

Three months without rain. Only the houseplants
    on the patio—in their terra cotta
pots—are watered, by hand,
    every other day. Last week, I watched
a young rat snake—gliding in
    exaggerated arcs—across the smooth
saltillo tile. Coiling into—a corner,
    to escape—the record-breaking heat.

        ****

But today, miraculously—by 6:00 a.m.—
    thunderheads stack—layers
upon layers—rumbling like distant
    cannon, and lightning streaks
the dawn. And then, slow large drops—
    of the blessèd rain—begin to fall,
spattering on metal gutters and eavespouts
    in punctuated rhythms.

I sit in a white wicker chair, my left
    foot propped on the small wicker table.
Drink my first cup—of coffee. I close
    my right eye, open my blind left
—hear the morning-song—rain—

Counter-point, the silken streams—
    slipping down—of a three-tiered, cast-iron
fountain. On the highest tier, two lovers
    shelter, under a wide-grooved umbrella.

Water wells up—
        spills—down the channels of this
umbrella, falling musically—into—the second
        tier. Then falls, finally—into—the third.

It has been raining—for over an hour, a
        silver spindrift of rain. And the misting from
the fountain—graces all the plants with
        glistening beads of water that—cluster around
the fountain and spill—across the saltillo tile.

Names slowly begin to swim—back to me.
        Long-fingered philodendron.
Chinese evergreen. A dwarf hibiscus
        bursting in coral blooms. A few
Latin words twist awkwardly off—my tongue
        like exaggerated postures from
the Kama Sutra—dracena, dieffenbachia,
        spathiphyllum. The rain
has been falling—for over two hours.

                ****

I re-enter the house, trailing the left leg—
        pour another cup—of coffee.
I disinter a portable CD player from
        the flotsam—of the study closet and
trek back to the patio—I insert Vivaldi, push
        repeat twice—immerse in four-trumpet concerti.

Antonio lays theme—upon evolving theme,
        and they jostle and shoulder
one another toward the dominance of
        a solo trumpet. The solitary notes invoke—
an intricate baroque—building into
        an inevitable finality. It has already been raining—
steadily, gently, exquisitely—for three hours.

                ****

My wife's love—deep to the marrow,
        my teenage daughter's
constellation-filled eyes—

72

the counter-point music
of the three-tiered fountain—
    the high-soaring, over-scoring trumpet:
All this—just this—is more than enough.
    And if another stroke should take me
this very night, I lived a blesséd life
    —and the rain just keeps falling.

What My Grandfather Said

A little rain on the roof,
enough money to pay the bills,
a measure of work
to dignify the spirit,
a good woman,
and children.

That's all there is.
That's all there ever was.

41531303R00052

Made in the USA
Lexington, KY
21 May 2015